Year of Our Lord

FAITH, HOPE, AND HARMONY IN THE MISSISSIPPI DELTA

PHOTOGRAPHS BY
Langdon Clay

TEXT BY
T.R. Pearson

Mockingbird Publishing
Fairhope, Alabama

Light rises in the darkness for the upright.

—PSALMS 112:4

Contents

What Do You Know About Jesus?

Lucas McCarty sings in the choir of the Trinity House of Prayer in Moorhead, Mississippi. Even by unexacting Delta standards, this country church is an eccentric affair. The building occupies an expansive open lot opposite a rice field. There is no proper sign, no steeple, not even a cross by way of identification. Though the tin church roof is new and forest green, most everything else is faded and sun-warped, particularly the blistered window frames which appear to cling to their red plastic panes through a blend of divine will and artless caulking.

The gravel parking lot is bordered on two sides by a fleet of abandoned vehicles—trucks and vans, a rusting church bus, a trio of tractors, a decrepit motor home with all of its windows broken out. The assortment is mired and half hidden in weeds and uncropped fescue, and the general state of the place, grounds and building taken together, suggests a flagging rear action against climate and circumstance. Each piecemeal stab at upkeep has been countered and undone by the swarming fertility of the Mississippi Delta, by the punishing sun and humidity, by the irrepressible local verdure.

Sunday services at the Trinity House of Prayer begin in the vicinity of noon and tend to run in excess of three hours. The church is unaffiliated with any established denomination. Trinity is sanctified. Except for Lucas McCarty, the congregation is black.

On the June Sunday I first laid eyes on Lucas in the Trinity parking lot, he was twenty years old. Complications attending his birth starved him of oxygen, and the ensuing brain trauma—commonly known as cerebral palsy—had left Lucas in limited control of his muscles. His movements are abrupt and spastic. He jerks and flails, twitches and drools, and is incapable of anything approaching the fluid, directed motion most of us manage unthinkingly when we pluck up a fork or turn a doorknob. Lucas can't speak. His voice is a moist, inarticulate growl. Though he uses a wheelchair occasionally, Lucas prefers to walk on his knees.

I followed him into his church through a back door and down a narrow back hallway to the sanctuary proper. The Trinity House of Prayer might look ramshackle on the outside, but the interior is handsome and well appointed. The carpet and pew cushions are a vivid scarlet. The woodwork, all knotty pine, has been lacquered to a high sheen, and the altar is freighted with an ambitious assortment of bright-brass, liturgical bric-a-brac.

Lucas ushered me to the deacons' bench, an all too conspicuous place of honor flanking the altar, and abandoned me there to make his way toward the choir loft. He climbed the stairs on his knees and parked himself at the front rail as the band members took their places. The drummer and organist were teenagers, young men who turned out to be cousins. The guitar player, his massive hands about the size of dinner plates, plucked at his ivory Stratocaster while the bassist adjusted his amp.

To kick off the service, the band embarked a little raggedly on "What Do You Know About Jesus?" but had settled into a proper groove by the time the choir began to file in from the narthex. It was a ladies' choir, one dozen strong. The women wore their Sunday best instead of robes, and the congregation rose to sing and clap along as the choir advanced up the center aisle toward the altar.

Lucas was singing too. He served as a kind of vocal baseline, a moaning foundation low and persistent beneath the lyrics. "Aaaaaaayyyyy." He was visible from the sternum up behind the choir rail. His arms were raised. His eyes were closed. Lucas's swaying was jerky and fitful. He drooled as he sang. "Aaaaaaaaaayyyyyy."

The choir members circled the altar and climbed into the loft, still singing. "What do you know about Jesus? He's all right. He's all right." The guitarist laid down rapid-fire filigree while the drummer, a mere ten feet to my left, threw in the occasional rim shot that rang out like rifle fire. The organist was now both singing and directing the choir as he played. His voice was high, sweet, and pure.

Music filled the sanctuary, and there was an emphatic sense of rejoicing in the air. Trinity's bishop, a spry sixty-nine-year-old in an elegant mustard-colored suit, stalked across the riser to gather Lucas in an embrace over the choir rail.

The singing continued for nearly an hour, a blend of traditional hymns such as "Jesus, Keep Me Near the Cross" and contemporary gospel numbers, a sort of Christ-inflected R&B. The choir and band together produced an extraordinary caliber of music, far removed from the weekly soprano death match I'd endured in my youth among the suburban Methodists.

Announcements followed the singing. Birthdays were recognized. Guests were invited to stand, and then Deacons Groves and Minton, my pewmates, rose to conduct the offertory. Instead of passing plates, two dishes were presented on a small table before the pulpit. One was for contributions to Trinity's mortgage—what Deacon Groves called "the note"—the other to help fund Trinity's weekly radio broadcast. The congregation filed past pew by pew, followed by the ladies' choir and Lucas, who negotiated his way out of the loft and around the altar on his knees. No one exhibited the least reluctance to make change from the dishes.

Deacon Groves consecrated the offering with a prayer that yielded to song. There were shouts of praise throughout the sanctuary and enough wailing in tongues to suggest the service might veer altogether into lively, unscripted territory. As Sister Hermenia, the bishop's niece, took the floor to receive testimony, Lucas came kneewalking out of the choir loft and clambered up onto the pew beside me. A woman across the sanctuary began to speak in clinical detail of a skin condition she'd relieved by "praying through." Sister Hermenia then embarked upon a prayer that soon ascended from excited to something approaching hysterical. Many in the sanctuary began wailing and speaking in tongues.

15

The bishop rose from his chair on the altar. He took up a bottle of Pompeii olive oil from a ledge by the pulpit and anointed his hands. With an assistant in tow, he sought out the loudest, the most affected members and pressed his oily palm to their foreheads. The assistant, a solitary hand raised, caught them as they dropped, slain by the spirit.

The sanctuary was in a general uproar. There were shouts and cries from every quarter of the place. Lucas contributed a pulsing "ehahhh." The whole scene was so exotic and alien to me that I couldn't decide if things were coming entirely apart or falling rapturously together.

Once the bishop had returned to the pulpit and wiped the olive oil off his hands, the fever seemed to ebb. There was weeping here and there and prayerful murmuring. Bishop Willie B. Knighten gripped the pulpit and embarked upon his sermon with the words, "I won't keep you long today."

For the next hour and a half, the bishop worked an improvisation on a chunk of Leviticus that was by turns stirring, funny, illuminating, wrong-headed, tender, harsh, and incomprehensible. His stamina was Castro-like. From a front pew, a young woman read a verse of the text when called upon which would reliably touch off an interpretive peroration from Bishop Knighten replete with vaguely related tangents and lively offshoots. The sermon's general thrust hewed to the worldly challenges of living holy, but the bishop strayed to indulge in a critique of rap music, the considerable difference between "saints and ain'ts," the sin of homosexuality, and the boundless value of Christian charity for the downtrodden.

Two teens having a side chat deep in the sanctuary briefly snared the bishop's attention. "I'll stop preaching and start fighting," he told them. The young men shriveled into blessed silence. To the rest of us, the bishop added, "I don't want to keep you," as preamble to another forty-five minutes of sermonizing.

It was a remarkable performance. Though the congregation was decidedly blue collar and black, the tone and theme of the bishop's remarks were positively Republican. If the sermon had a subtext, it was *get off your sorry ass and do right*. Women were to serve. Children were to obey. And men were to love and lead. This was the Old Testament as brittle prescription.

But the people the bishop was preaching to, was hectoring even every now and again, had no hard moral edges to them. There was no sense of judgment afoot in the place. The challenge of living up to the demands of the Gospel and the expectations of the Lord appeared to be embraced among the membership as a happy privilege rather than shouldered as a chore.

Children made up about a third of the congregation, and they shifted among pews during the course of the sermon, moving discreetly through the sanctuary, parking for a while with one congenial adult or another and then traveling on. Aside from the two boys whispering, everyone was impeccably behaved for very nearly four hours.

Then there was the care the congregation showered on Lucas, separate from the service but ongoing throughout it. Lucas was kept supplied with paper towels to wipe the drool from his chin. When he needed water, he signaled the organist, who operated the fountain for him. A child in his Sunday suit, while touring the sanctuary, made Lucas one of his stops and perched beside him for a while. This was before the sermon had worn Lucas down and he dropped off to sleep.

He didn't just doze. Lucas fell into a profound slumber and lounged against me for the better part of an hour. I feared he would topple off the pew or drool all over my sport coat. I feared, in fact, each equally. I was probably less at ease with Lucas than anybody else in the church. Without exception, Trinity's members treated Lucas with unstudied compassion. Instead of thinking Lucas diminished by his condition, his friends at Trinity seemed to consider him blessed by it, almost anointed.

Early on, just before the service began, Deacon Groves had caught me watching Lucas struggling into the choir loft. I was feeling pity primarily, which must have showed. "God," the deacon told me, "never makes a mistake."

Announcements followed the sermon. I was a little staggered to hear there was an evening service in a Greenville church many in the congregation were planning to attend and over which the bishop would preside. After a quick benediction (and one final offering), we were finally excused. It was ten minutes to 4:00.

The bishop stepped over to speak to me. He'd donned a dapper bowler hat, hardly standard clerical attire. But then the bishop didn't much look like a peace-be-upon-you sort of guy. He may have been crowding seventy, but he was solid and broad-shouldered and had enough mischief to him—in his gaze, in his remarks—to seem entirely capable of coaxing Jesus into a fellow or, failing that, throttling the devil out of him.

I followed Lucas as he knee-walked between the drum kit and the choir loft. He swung open the door at the far end of the back hallway and waited for me to take an arm and squire him into the afternoon sun.

Locked Up in There

Lucas McCarty was born in Woman's Hospital in Flowood, Mississippi, on the seventh of February, 1986. His discharge summary reads in part, "The baby delivered with no heart rate, no tone and no spontaneous respiration." Two and a half years later, an evaluation at the Memphis campus of the University of Tennessee resulted in the catchall diagnosis "developmental delay." According to the report, Lucas had "some jargon but no recognizable or meaningful speech sounds."

Lucas's history—medical, educational, therapeutic, and photographic—resides tidily in a pair of blue ring binders that have been curated through the years by his mother. "I couldn't keep things straight in my mind," she told me.

Elizabeth McCarty is a school teacher by profession. She is practical, unflappable, and devoted to her son. Of the complications attending Lucas's birth, Elizabeth said, "They just didn't get him out fast enough." A lawsuit against the obstetrician came to nothing, and the vagueness of Lucas's diagnosis sustained Elizabeth in her faith that, with proper treatment, Lucas might well improve, might even recover. "I just wanted to help him," she said. "I'd cling to anything."

Elizabeth pursued every available therapeutic avenue to little measurable effect. The sheer, desperate effort of it all tore at her marriage and, ultimately, helped dissolve it.

"We dealt with what went on with Lucas in different ways," Lucas's father told me. Chuck McCarty owns and operates a restaurant in Indianola. He and Elizabeth separated three years after Lucas's birth and divorced three years after that. "I think Elizabeth was always looking for the magic pill, and it just wasn't there."

The final straw for Chuck McCarty came in the form of a trip to Philadelphia's Institutes for the Achievement of Human Potential. Founded by Glenn Doman (a physical therapist) and Carl Delacato (an educational psychologist), the Institute promotes the practice of "patterning," a therapy designed to train the compromised brain through repeated patterns of movement. "That was one of the worst weeks of my life," Chuck McCarty said. "We went to class from six in the morning until nine or ten at night in a freezing cold room because, according to them, your brain works better when it's cold." Chuck McCarty remains convinced his didn't.

The staff spent the bulk of their time instructing the parents in how to move and manipulate their children to help them crawl their way out of their neurological difficulties. Parents were expected to spend many hours a day physically positioning their children's limbs. In the literature of the Institute—carefully preserved in one of Elizabeth's blue binders—any failure of the therapy is laid with cruel convenience to a lack of diligence on the part of the parents. Even twenty years later, the built-in guilt has lost little of its potency. "Maybe we didn't stick with patterning long enough," Chuck McCarty told me.

Even today there's no reliable measure of intellect for a child in Lucas McCarty's condition, no useful IQ test for a non-reading, non-speaking subject. Certainly cerebral palsy can be attended by severe mental retardation, but it doesn't have to be, and Elizabeth McCarty had a mother's sense that her son was "locked up in there," she called it. The key was to find some way to let him out.

Lucas could sign for necessities, but his signing vocabulary was sparse and, given his contracted muscles, he was likely to become less nimble over time rather than more so. Worse still, a signer requires a signee. Elizabeth wanted to equip Lucas with the means to speak to anybody about anything at any time.

There were few options on that front when Lucas was a child, the most promising being an icon-based language called Minspeak. The brainchild of classical linguist Bruce Baker, Minspeak was a relatively new addition to the world of assisted communication. Baker had created it in the summer of 1980. He had been studying social attitudes toward people with disabilities as expressed in language.

"I had taught a boy with cerebral palsy to drive," Baker told me. "He had mild CP, but people still made all sorts of horrendous remarks about him."

In the course of his research, Baker had met a number of cerebral palsy sufferers who were making do with primitive communication aids. "There was an old man with a revolving metal disc," Baker recalled. "It had numbers and letters enameled around it. When he got to a letter he wanted, he'd hit a switch rigged to a typewriter. Communication was so slow as to be virtually impossible." Baker had also come across a woman dependent on a head stick to make her wishes known. "She had a picture of a toilet on the lapboard of her wheelchair," Baker said. "So her full range of communication was toilet or not toilet. Period."

Baker's challenge was to create and deploy a language that took a user's restricted movement into account. The spell-to-speech approach called not just for full literacy but the dexterity to strike every letter on a keyboard, which left a whole swathe of potential users unserved. What of those people whose conditions had kept them from proper schooling, the sort who could sustain directed motion only erratically and laboriously at best? Conventional typing was out of the question for them. The task was to somehow marry rich, rhetorical potential with no need for literacy and the fewest keystrokes possible.

To that end, Baker conceived a language based on icons rather than letters. "Being a classics major, I'd had to learn the rudiments of Egyptian hieroglyphics and Mayan hieroglyphs," Baker said, "and I soon discovered I could represent with fifty icons virtually any word imaginable." Better still, he could do it with the sort of economy restricted movement demanded.

In Minspeak, for example, if a user wants to say the word "bedroom," he combines two icons, which are merely cartoon pictures on individual keyboard keys. The first is a picture of a bed. The second a picture of a map—the what and the where. In combination, two keystrokes produce a word that, if typed, would require seven. Entire sentences that might call for dozens of keystrokes in typed English can be accomplished in Minspeak with a fraction of the effort and no loss in fluency. "About eighty percent of the words we use daily are drawn from a core of fewer than four hundred words," Baker pointed out, "and that core vocabulary is consistent across populations, activities, places, topics—you name it."

Minspeak is a distinct language with its own rationale and idiosyncrasies, and like any language it has to be learned. And taught. Once Elizabeth McCarty had discovered

23

Minspeak and had secured for Lucas a Prentke Romich Delta Talker—one of the early Minspeak devices—she and Chuck McCarty received only an afternoon's worth of training on the thing before they carried it to their son, who failed to take up the Delta Talker with any enthusiasm.

By this time, Lucas was approaching school age, and his mother had decided to move north to Shelby County, Tennessee, where the special education program in the public school system far outstripped anything Indianola could offer. The family—Lucas, Elizabeth, and Lucas's sister, Elissa—relocated to Germantown just east of Memphis, and Lucas became a student who was "included in everything," his mother recalled, "from Boy Scouts, to putting on plays, to singing in the choir."

Lucas's schooling was managed primarily by teachers' aides, and his early education in Minspeak came at the hands of Lynne Shields. She'd recently given over her assembly line job at an air conditioning plant to work at Farmington Elementary School in Memphis. "I'd never been around people with disabilities," Lynne confessed. "Lucas was my very first student."

At this point, Lynne knew little more about Minspeak than Lucas did. "We learned together," Lynne said. "I had his Delta Talker instruction manual that I'd take home at night. Lucas and I just winged it. We tried to talk about stuff he liked."

The stuff Lucas liked fell into two distinct categories: house cleaning and black people. Apparently, Lucas was born with a passion for vacuuming. "He came into the world cleaning," Elizabeth McCarty told me. "He wanted a vacuum when he was probably a year old." It's an enthusiasm that hasn't flagged in two decades. Lucas's favorite literature remains janitorial supply catalogs, and he'll fairly swoon over a state-of-the-art Electrolux in the fashion most young men reserve for Lamborghinis.

If he didn't come into the world with an affection for people of color as well, Lucas surely acquired it early on. While flipping through one of Elizabeth McCarty's binders, I turned up several photographs taken on a family trip to Orlando. Lucas must have been three or four years old at the time. These weren't pictures of Space Mountain or the Country Bear Jamboree. Instead they were snapshots of Lucas in the company of several black m19 from his hotel. Likely he was attracted by their equipment and their occupation, but there was something in themselves he was drawn to as well.

"Lucas always told me black people are more real," Lynne Shields recalled. "They talk to him like a regular person." While I'd noticed the easy rapport Lucas enjoys in his church, I'd laid it off to familiarity, but when I asked Bruce Baker if he'd ever remarked a difference in the way white people and black people respond to the disabled, he was quick to assure me he had. "Every Darwinian fiber in our brain is wanting to note the differences when we see a disabled person," Baker told me, "but you and I were taught not to stare. I think black people are less uptight in general and less plagued by these what-are-other-people-going-to-think moms."

There's certainly something at work that Lucas sensed and embraced early on. I've had occasion now to see gaggles of white folks gawking at Lucas from safe distances as he pitches out of his wheelchair and negotiates terrain on his knees, and I have watched a lone black gentleman—a stranger to Lucas—cross an entire parking lot to lay a hand to Lucas's shoulder and tell him hello. Two peoples propelled by the same nugget of Scripture—*there but for the grace of God*—in opposite directions.

"I am," Lucas has told me more than once, "white on the outside but black on the inside."

Since Lucas's mother considered the move to the Memphis suburbs strategic and temporary, she'd kept her house in Indianola, which the family returned to most weekends. Lucas might have been struggling to learn Minspeak, but he was already fully conversant in gospel music and had begun to collect recordings that he'd listen to Sunday mornings as a warm up for service at the family's place of worship, St. Stephen's Episcopal Church. By native disposition, Lucas was about as far from Episcopalian as a fellow can get, so when an invitation came his way to attend a black holiness church, he was more than ready to leave St. Stephen's behind.

Brother John Woods carried Lucas to his first service at the Trinity House of Prayer. Woods worked at the time (and still does) for Elizabeth McCarty's father, Jimmy Lear, who owns and operates a catfish farm near the Delta community of Sunflower. John Woods is what's known in the region as an oxygen man. Delta catfish are raised in clusters of ten-to-fifteen-acre rectangular ponds and spend their brief lives—from fingerling to harvest-ready adult—in about four feet of water.

From May to October—in the punishing, evaporative heat of the Delta—the shallow ponds can become oxygen depleted. If the oxygen level of the water drops to four parts per million, the catfish will surface to breathe. If it falls to two parts per million, every fish in the pond will die, usually within thirty minutes. The danger is greatest in the small hours of the night, and since the cost of a lost pond can run into the hundreds of thousands of

25

dollars, the oxygen man must be a person of impeccable reliability. The success of the entire operation depends upon him.

Many Delta catfish farmers protect their investment by serving as their own oxygen men or hiring bonded fish management companies to the do the job for them. Lucas's grandfather relies on John Woods who, from early spring through autumn, visits Jimmy Lear's ponds almost hourly throughout each night to take a measure of things with a probe at the end of a telescoping pole. If the water registers oxygen-starved, Woods engages paddle wheels—some floating, others tractor driven—to churn up the water and replenish it.

Occasionally, young Lucas McCarty rode with John Woods on his evening rounds. "Even though Lucas was going to the Episcopal church at the time," Woods said, "I could tell he kind of leaned toward black folks."

In those days, Woods was the director of music at the Trinity House of Prayer, and with the family's permission, John Woods began to carry Lucas to the church. Not just on Sundays but throughout the week as well. "We'd go by ourselves," Woods told me. "We'd hold hands and pray. And we'd have to sing some songs. Lucas loves to sing."

Lucas began attending Sunday service with John Woods and his wife, Mary Frances. "He'd scoot all the way to the choir stand," Mary Frances said, "and sit himself in the front row." Rather than objecting, the choir embraced Lucas, as did the bishop and the congregation, and Lucas knew he'd found a home. He soon began talking of joining the church as a proper member. "I asked him why he had to join Trinity," Lucas's father told me. "And he said, 'It's the only place that accepts me like I am.' Lucas said he wanted his name in the book, on the roll. And you can be sure no white church was going to let him sing in their choir. Not a chance."

The bond between Lucas and John Woods had soon become so profound that Lucas took to thinking of and referring to Woods as his "black daddy."

"I'm Lucas's spiritual father," John Woods told me when I met him and Mary Frances at Lucas's Indianola home. Woods parked himself at the piano and, in between hymns, noodled on the keys as he spoke of the history he and Lucas had enjoyed together, the friendship they'd developed. "Lucas is closer to God than you and me," he said. "We can walk and talk, help ourselves. Not him." John Woods then thundered out a rendition of "I've Got to Move to a Better Home" with Lucas joining in.

"Folks are watching you," Woods told Lucas, who was on his knees alongside the piano. "They're looking for the good or the bad, but I don't see no bad." John Woods then launched into "God's Got It All in Control" with "I'll Fly Away" following hard upon it. He spoke vaguely of the death of his son, of unnamed trouble in his past he'd overcome through Jesus. He spoke of a church he'd lately started in Belzoni, down the Delta. "We've brought a lot of backsliders to the Lord," Woods said as prelude to more noodling, more singing, and a final benediction delivered with his hand resting on Lucas's head.

Woods had an easy way with Lucas and Elizabeth, who'd come home from school to join us toward the end of Woods's stay. Once we'd seen John and Mary Frances out to their car, I passed along to Elizabeth some of what John Woods had told me, particularly the bit about his own dark past.

We were still waving from the driveway as Elizabeth said, "I think he killed a man."

God Ain't Told Me Nothing

It took me a full two weeks to find John Woods again. He sleeps days since he works nights, which left only a couple of hours in the morning and a couple in the evening when Woods was both unemployed and awake. I tried calling and leaving polite messages for a few days, but I eventually took to haunting Jimmy Lear's catfish ponds in the late afternoon and finally ran across John and Mary Frances on their rounds.

Woods was driving an old Chevy pickup truck, and I watched as he sent the thing plunging down a pond embankment only to veer parallel to the water at the last second. Mary Frances then shoved a telescoping probe out the passenger window, dipped the tip of it into the pond, and John gunned the engine and raced up the embankment while she noted the reading on a clipboard. As I waited across the way, they repeated this process seamlessly from pond to pond, a pure necessity given that they had eighty-nine to cover.

Naturally, John Woods could only spare a couple of minutes for me, and we made an appointment for the following Friday evening when he was off work. Lucas insisted on coming along, and he served as my navigator as we went looking for John Woods's house off the main street in Moorhead. It was late spring, and the night was still and buggy. There was thunder to the west. In such weather, the Mississippi Delta is about as mosquito plagued and fly blown as the Amazon basin. That was hardly enough, however, to keep John and Mary Frances's neighbors off the street.

I'd noticed that people do a lot of living out of doors in the Delta, and come evening you can often find whole neighborhoods in the road. The children playing, the parents visiting. John's street was fairly thronged as Lucas and I rolled through the crowd until Lucas told me, "Ehhh," and gestured toward a tidy white house with a fenced in front yard.

John came out to help me bring Lucas inside, and we ushered him between us to the front door where Lucas went to his knees, walked across the carpet, and climbed onto the sofa. John Woods's large oak desk dominated the room. An electric keyboard rested upon it, and John played a few minor chords as I acquainted him with what little I'd learned of his past since I'd met him. Lucas's grandfather—Chuck's father, Alvin McCarty— had told me, "I've been knowing John Woods forever, before he got saved, when he used to be a drunk. I knew him when he got in trouble, when he killed that man."

I asked John if he would tell me about it, all of it. "All right," he said and switched off his keyboard. "I got saved," John Woods began, "in nineteen eighty-seven. During that same year, I made tragedy in my life."

On Father's Day in 1987 my brother LeRoy came to my house, to this house, and told me that Johnny, our brother-in-law, had knocked my sister in the head with a pipe. I had a .38 pistol back in a drawer. One thing about a weapon—it's made to kill, and once a person has a gun in his hand, things you wouldn't normally do, you will do. A weapon takes fear out of a man's heart.

We went down to Moorhead, me and LeRoy, and found Johnny in a cafe. It was Sunday morning—I'll never forget it—and he was drinking a tall can of beer. I was just going to jump on him right there, but when I saw him, God did something to my heart. I told Johnny that him and my sister should maybe separate for a while. Then me and LeRoy got in our truck and left.

A car came up behind us, blowing the horn. It was Johnny. He pulled up right beside us and told us he had something for us. Johnny raised a pistol, a little .25 automatic, and LeRoy ran into the ditch. Johnny fired two shots—Pow! Pow!—and then nothing. I peeked out and saw that Johnny's gun had jammed.

He was working the thing and just getting a bullet in the chamber when I raised my gun and pulled the trigger. As soon as I did, I knew my life had changed. I hadn't even aimed, just fired, but it got real quiet, and I knew. I knew.

Sure enough, there was a hole in Johnny's head. I just started trembling, and LeRoy brought me home.

Back then, I wasn't saved, but Mary Frances was. I was still drinking and smoking dope.

I told Mary Frances what I'd done, and I asked her what I should do about it. I said I could go to New York, up to Jamaica where I had people. Then the thought came to my mind, and I asked her to pray for me. I'd never asked her to do that before. We got on our knees, and she cried to the Lord on my behalf. I felt peace come into my heart, and I decided I should just wait for the sheriff.

The deputy pulled up in my driveway. I knew him well. He told me they had to cuff me and take me in. They carried me to the courthouse, where I wrote out my statement. Then they took me upstairs and locked me up. Put me in a cell, and I didn't know what to do. When you shoot somebody, you can't take it back.

Bishop Knighten's sister worked at the jail, and she came to my cell and told me Johnny had died on the way to Jackson. I remember she said, "Baby, God has got his hands on you."

My cellmate was a backslider. He'd been a preacher, but he was in for hitting his child. He told me to tell my story to God. Tell Him how I felt. Tell Him I was sorry. But I didn't see what I'd done as murder. I didn't think I needed God to forgive me. That's how you think when you're not saved.

In the middle of the night, I got out of my bunk, went to my knees, and folded my hands in prayer. The only thing I said was, "God, if You're up there, will You please help me?" I was a stiff-hearted person. When my mother died, I didn't even cry. I was usually high on marijuana. But there in that jail cell, I started crying. I felt a presence in there, something I'd never felt before.

I was scared to move. When the spirit began to touch me it was like warm oil running down my body. All of a sudden, I found myself smiling. The backslider woke up and looked down at me. He said, "You don't need to tell me what happened. I can see it." I threw away my cigarettes, my dope. Never had either one since.

They charged me with murder one. A fellow I used to work for hired a lawyer for me, a man named Joe Buchanan. They ended up trying me twice. The first time was in 1988, and the jury was hung. For the second trial, they reduced the charge to manslaughter. My lawyer was nervous, but I told him God had talked to me, and He said He was going to set me free.

I'll never forget this. My lawyer, Joe Buchanan, he laughed and said, "I sure hope so because God ain't told me nothing."

The D.A. was a lady. She was tough and had the bluest eyes I'd ever seen. She said I'd hunted down my brother-in-law like a dog. Joe told the jury I was innocent, and he cried, I remember, cried like a baby.

When the jury came in, they handed the verdict to the judge, and the judge looked at me—seemed like forever—and told me the jury had found me not guilty. It was all because of the grace of God. He knows everything in advance. He knew we'd meet Lucas McCarty, and He knew Lucas would need fellowship. Didn't He?

From his perch on the sofa, Lucas waved both of his arms in the air as he told John Woods, "Eeeahhh!" John switched on his keyboard and embarked on a full-throated version of "I Belong to the King." The storm was just above us by now, the rain pouring down. Lucas harmonized after his fashion, moaning tunefully, lowly, as John Woods played and sang.

> I belong to the King
> I belong to the King
> Jesus is my savior
> I belong to the King

Cottonlandia

Though Lucas is a fully accomplished Minspeak success story today, he didn't take to his Delta Talker or have much practical use for the language for several years after he'd started school. "Lucas only used the talker as a school activity," Lynne Shields recalled. "It was work in his mind. He didn't even take it home with him."

Lynne babysat for Lucas occasionally, so she had a full sense of what he was up to in and out of school. "He wasn't ever much of a TV watcher," Lynne said. "He had no interest in reading or math. Lucas was just interested in life."

When Lucas graduated to the sixth grade, he came into the sphere of a new teacher's aide, a woman named Patty Mulford, who had never seen a Delta Talker before Lucas brought his to class. Mulford was obliged to attend seminars conducted by a county speech therapist to get some sense of what Minspeak was all about.

"Because we had to feed him with our fingers," Patty Mulford told me, "he ate in the classroom, and I fed him. So there I was stuck with Lucas, and I just started talking to him like he was a regular kid." And he was a regular kid in all the ways that mattered, though maybe more contentious than most. "Boy," Mulford said, "did he love to argue. He'd come in here and say, 'If you're not a Christian and you don't believe in God, you're going to hell.' And I'd say, 'No you're not.' And off we'd go."

After several years of indifferent progress on his Delta Talker, Lucas found in Patty Mulford someone who could finally goad him into fluency. "He fixated on religion," Mulford said. "Who's going to hell and who's not. What's a sin and what's not. It got to the point where the teachers were fighting with each other about it. Then he told me hard-headed people went to hell, and I couldn't let that go. I'm pretty hard-headed."

Lucas *had* to learn to talk. How else could he quarrel with Patty Mulford? She made Lucas use Minspeak to write a full-page journal entry every day on his Delta Talker. He'd write about places he'd like to visit, things he'd like to do. "My son had a shop, and sometimes I'd take Lucas over there, and he'd wind up all of the electrical chords. He's about as obsessive-compulsive as they come." He'd write about cleaning. He'd write about heaven and hell. "Lucas always had great spirit and curiosity," Patty Mulford told me. "His mother saw it. I kind of gravitated toward her. Elizabeth knew what was important."

Once Lucas passed out of middle school, however, and into high school, everything changed. "It all stopped," Patty Mulford said. "The feeling was 'if he can't read, he can't be here,'" and Lucas was literate only in Minspeak. Reading and writing standard English had never held any interest for him. Worse still, Lucas's high school teachers focused on activities that struck Elizabeth as a little idiotic. "They made him put on his coat. It took maybe an hour, sometimes an hour and a half. What's the point? To me that's just cruel and stupid."

In all, the family spent eleven years in the Memphis suburb of Germantown but finally moved back to Indianola once it became clear to Elizabeth McCarty that Lucas's schooling had become unacademic. His teachers and his aides were now focusing exclusively on functional living. "It was all shoe tying," Elizabeth told me, "and washing off tables."

So the McCartys returned to their Indianola home. Elizabeth took a teaching job at a school nearby. Elissa, Lucas's sister, went off to college in eastern Tennessee, and Lucas stayed home most days in the company of the family's longtime housekeeper and unofficial nanny who'd been with the McCartys and Lears since well before Lucas's birth. This was essentially the Lucas I met on that Sunday in June. Not yet twenty-one and properly adult. Chafing against grinding idleness. Ambitions dormant. Not despairing but by no means satisfied. In short, emblematic of the Mississippi Delta at large.

There's a distinct air of stifled potential among the general population of the Delta. Nagging joblessness is a leading feature of the place. New efficiencies in farming, while improving yields and enhancing profits, have simultaneously closed off opportunities for employment. More acreage than ever is now farmed in the Delta with fewer hands than have ever been needed to farm it.

I had the good fortune one evening of meeting a proper Delta planter in the bar of the Alluvian Hotel in Greenwood. Walter Pitts grew up in a farming family north of Indianola and has continued the tradition with his siblings. While I was sensible of the scope and magnitude of Delta agriculture, I couldn't begin to wrap my mind around how it was all managed and by whom. Though Pitts was politely reluctant at first—talking farming is a little like talking money—I eventually wore him down and managed to pump him for information both that evening and the following afternoon at his home.

Here is what struck me as the essential fact of the new Mississippi Delta: Walter Pitts and his brothers and sisters farm nearly ten thousand acres of land with a grand total of eleven people, all of them tractor drivers.

"When I came home from college to farm," Walter Pitts told me, "we had twenty-six tractors on three thousand acres. You used to have to plow cotton four or five times. Now you just use Roundup." It's a different game today with entirely different equipment. "The tractors look like jets anymore," Pitts said. "I got up on one the other day and was going to move it, but there were so many switches and buttons, I couldn't do it."

In the summer of 2007, when I spoke to Walter Pitts, his family was growing primarily soybeans and corn, a little over four thousand acres of each. Historically, the Delta has been cotton rich, but no more. "It's all going to India and Pakistan," Pitts said, "where labor is cheap and they can use any chemical they want to." Since the low market price of cotton these days can hardly begin to compensate a Delta farmer for the considerable expense of growing it, a driving tour through the modern-day Delta turns up only the occasional cotton field.

"I'm not going to sit here and lose my farm just because I'm a cotton farmer," Pitts told me. "Cotton is down to fifty cents a pound, which was the price when my father was farming."

Soybeans and corn now dominate the Delta, but there is a considerable amount of wheat as well. "It's the easiest thing to grow around here," Pitts told me. "You plant it and water it one time." Soybeans are probably the next most forgiving crop with corn closing

45

due to a recently introduced Roundup-resistant strain. "Now we can just spray the herbicide on top of it," Pitts said. "That makes everything easier, and you've got to do whatever you can. Farming's a funny business," Pitts added. "Farmers buy retail and sell wholesale. Everybody else does it the other way around."

Walter Pitts then fished a remarkable book out of a cabinet in his den, a portfolio-sized USDA soil survey published originally in the 1940s. The Department of Agriculture of the day had dispatched a team of soil testers across the Delta. They'd traveled in phalanx and on foot, taking soil samples every ten to fifteen yards. The men categorized the dirt by rubbing it between their fingers to gauge granularity. "They named it by listening to it," Walter Pitts told me and then showed me a plat including a sizable stretch of acreage farmed by the Pitts family. The various strains of soil, scores of them, were depicted as topographical fingers of earth in shifting shades of gray.

Each distinct type of dirt was named for a town in the Delta. "Dubbs silty loam," Pitts said, pointing out a streak of soil on the plat. "That's your best soil in this part of the country. Not pure sand but sand with a little clay in it—loamy. The general quality of the soil around here depends on how the river ran thousands of years ago."

Before the levee system was completed, the Mississippi River ran in flood almost anywhere it pleased and submerged the Delta with some regularity. Technically the Mississippi Delta isn't a delta at all. It's a seven-thousand-square-mile alluvial plain that lies between the Yazoo and Mississippi River basins and covers nearly two hundred miles north to south and seventy miles across at its widest point. Eons of flooding have washed most of the sand from the Delta soil, and the vast bulk of it has the look of black loam, the sort you might pour from a potting soil bag. "The Delta, the Nile Valley, and the San Joaquin Valley," Walter Pitts told me as he carefully packed his soil survey book away, "are the richest farming lands on earth."

The last great Delta flood occurred in 1927. Since then, Delta farmers have steadily improved their yields with the ongoing evolution of equipment and engineered seed, irrigation technologies, nutrients, pesticides, and herbicides. In the 1940s, an acre of Delta land might have produced ten to fifteen bushels of soybeans. Now, in a good year, eighty to ninety bushels per acre isn't uncommon. These advances, naturally enough, haven't come without a price.

The whole structure of farming in the Delta is incessantly getting rejiggered and renovated. Initially labor fueled the Delta's success. Cotton was planted and chopped and harvested by slaves, then emancipated slaves, and then imported labor from all over the earth. In the wake of the Civil War when freed men could give over the trials of cotton farming if they chose to, much of the Delta's black population drifted north to Chicago and Detroit, and Delta planters actively recruited replacements from eastern Europe, from Italy, from Central America, from the Middle and Far East. By the 1920s the first mechanical cotton picker—a single-row contraption—had appeared in the fields and was capable of replacing forty hand laborers. Now massive combines and multirow spindle pickers harvest all of the crops in the Delta.

The agricultural evolution of the Delta has, to a great extent, made the place what it is today—which is to say more than a little odd and wholly unexpected. Much of the South, particularly the Deep South, is surpassingly homogenous. White natives. Black natives. Small pockets of (mostly Latino) immigrants. The occasional snowbird from the upper midwest mystified by head cheese, hominy, and the territorial dearth of bratwurst.

I'm a North Carolinian by birth, a Virginian by residence, and I had long considered myself an unimpeachable Southerner until I stopped in a diner in the wilds of northern Alabama on one of my trips to the Delta. This was the sort of place with lard in the biscuits and fried bologna on the menu. My waitress proved chatty, nosy in fact. She'd never laid eyes on me before and knew it.

"Where are you from, hon?" she asked me.

I told her.

"That's nice." She topped off my coffee and smiled. "We like outsiders," she said.

Outsiders? This was Alabama, for goodness sakes, not Albania. But that is the South in its essence: clannish and always mindful of who exactly is *us* and who precisely is *them*. Due to its curious history, the Mississippi Delta turns this sort of parochialism on its head. Everywhere in the Delta, from the eastern hills to the great river, us *is* them. The Delta isn't remotely like the rest of the South. Culturally, it doesn't even resemble the rest of Mississippi. The place is curiously international and weirdly diverse. In the Delta, there are no outsiders.

I distinctly recall stepping into a grocery mart near Tchula, Mississippi, on one of my first Delta visits to be greeted by the owner behind the register. The man looked implacably Chinese. "Hey y'all," he told me with a drawl that would have put Gomer Pyle in the shade. Some of the best kibbe and baba ganoush this side of Damascus can be found in the northern Delta town of Clarksdale, where descendants of Lebanese laborers, recruited and

47

imported to pick cotton a century ago, have settled and stayed. Tamales remain a Delta staple many decades after their introduction by Mexican farm hands, and the marriage of Italian influence with traditional southern pig lust has resulted in barbecue spaghetti—part misguided culinary fusion, part spackle.

In the late nineteenth century, a full quarter of the population of the river city of Greenville (and two thirds of the merchant class) was German and Eastern European Jews. The Delta town of Cleveland had a one-room Chinese schoolhouse in the 1940s, and the namesake of both the city of Greenwood and the county it resides in is a half-blooded Choctaw Indian named Greenwood LeFlore who owned a one-thousand-acre plantation, four hundred slaves, and a grand home—*Malmaison*—famous for the opulence of its Louis XIV decor and the fire that destroyed it in 1942.

Unlike the bulk of the South, the Mississippi Delta has long been a stew pot of world ethnicity. White Delta planters were a minority from the beginning. In the mid-nineteenth century, the Delta's slave population outnumbered white landholders five to one. That ratio of black to white is closer to two to one today, but add in the imported ethnic mix that has accumulated in the Delta, both by design and by happenstance, and the residual white population of the area is nearly modest enough to constitute a cult.

This fact was brought home to me one afternoon when I stopped by a Belzoni grocery store, actually *the* Belzoni grocery store. It was choked with shoppers, and one check-out girl and I were the only Caucasians in the place. Most everyone else was black with a few Chinese and Latino customers in numbers that seemed to mirror the region's demographic at large.

The current mix isn't entirely due to historical racial and ethnic balances. The present-day Delta is doggedly depopulating. Farmers' children in particular are fleeing the Delta in sizable numbers. With plunging cotton prices and the passing of the paddle wheeler, there are portions of the region that have come to feel derelict and bypassed, particularly those communities backed up against the river between the Helena bridge to the north and the Vicksburg bridge to the South.

The city of Greenville, for instance, was once a thriving metropolis with regular steamboat traffic, an opera house, a city center of grand boulevards and neo-Roman architecture. On a recent weekday afternoon, I attracted local police attention by simply strolling around downtown Greenville. I was the lone pedestrian walking past blocks of shuttered storefronts and trudging from avenue to avenue, stunned by the scale and the desolation of the place. The citizens, as it turned out, were at the mall east of town or mired in the retail clottage along the approach from the north. Doubtless no few of them were parked in casinos on the far side of the levee.

A Greenville P.D. radio car eased to the curb ahead of me. A large pink-necked officer rolled out with a grunt. "How we doing?" he asked me.

We were hot. As is our custom, we were also about half lost. I said I was looking for a place to eat, and he directed me to a diner a couple of blocks over, assured me I'd know it by the cars out front. That seemed likely given that there were no cars anywhere else.

"Is it always like this?" I asked him.

"Like what?"

I was one of three patrons at Jim's Cafe. The food was cheap and delicious, and the walls were crowded with framed photographs of old Greenville, thriving cotton-rich Greenville, flooded Greenville. Once I'd eaten, I worked my way around the restaurant, taking in each picture while one of my fellow patrons held forth at appreciable length and to no one in particular on the battle of Thermopylae. He confessed to having little use for Persians.

I came away with a distinct sense of Greenville as a town in full ebb. Built for sixty or seventy thousand people, the city now boasts a population closer to forty thousand, and it loses an additional seven or eight hundred citizens every year. The city of Greenwood, forty-five minutes to the east, is in similar straits. At its peak, Greenwood was home to thirty-eight thousand souls. Today, that number is slightly over eighteen thousand. Unlike Greenville, however, revitalization has begun to take hold in Greenwood, thanks largely to Fred Carl, founder and CEO of the Viking Range Corporation.

Carl is a Greenwood native, and in addition to employing a thousand Delta residents at his plant just west of town, he has made a decisive investment in the community's rebirth. The corporate offices of Viking Range occupy renovated office space in the Cotton

Row section of the city on the banks of the Yazoo River, and with the support of Carl and his company, several blocks along Greenwood's main street now house uncommonly swanky enterprises by Delta standards. There are upscale cafes and restaurants, a bakery and espresso bar, an ambitious independent book store, and, anchoring it all, the Alluvian Hotel and Spa. All occupy refitted original buildings in keeping with Fred Carl's conscious bid not just to re-energize the place but to reclaim as well the charm and character of old Greenwood.

The city has become a destination of sorts, and weekends often find the hotel fully occupied, the restaurants crowded, the antique shops and bookstore choked with customers—no few of them having already been cited by the Mississippi State Police, who have transformed the straight, flat thirty-mile connector between Greenwood and the interstate into a speed trap gauntlet. Welcome to the Delta, y'all.

The problem in Greenwood is that the city extends well beyond where the revitalization ends. In the neglected quarters, the town is neighboring Greenville on a smaller scale. The businesses are failing or long boarded up, and most of Greenwood is derelict. It would be petty not to hope for Fred Carl's success but maybe a little foolish to expect it.

On the municipal signs surrounding the city, Greenwood is identified as "The Cotton Capital of the World," and in a perverse way it still is. South of town, along the Yazoo City road, a warehouse complex stores unsold cotton. Building after building, bale upon bale. Thousands of them, tens of thousands, held against the day when the price recovers, the nation of Pakistan collapses, the Chinese unionize, something.

In the countryside, the Delta might feel slightly less abandoned, but often a failing and unenterprising pall touches even the smallest communities and is difficult to ignore. Economic anemia has come to feel endemic to the Delta. A driving tour through the region, from town to town, has a kind of demoralizing sameness to it that is only lightly relieved by the colorful place names: Mound Bayou, Panther Burn, Itta Bena, Alligator, Onward, Bobo, Midnight, Quito, Coahoma, Rena Lara, Isola, Tippo, Nitta Yuma, Hard Cash, Moon.

The typical Delta community consists of a block or two of retail space, perhaps a town square. A few are well preserved, even thriving in their fashion. Sumner, for example, with its meticulously preserved courthouse—site of the notorious Emmett Till trial—and its modest cluster of shops has a strain of Magic Kingdom tidiness to it. The rambling frame houses across the bayou adjacent to town are shaded by massive live oaks. They look the epitome of gracious Delta living. Sumner, however, is very much the exception.

Far more common is a place like Thornton, just north of Yazoo City. I stayed for several weeks in a house near Thornton and knew many occasions to drive past it, through it, around it at all times of the day. To the east of Thornton lies the Hillside National Wildlife Reservoir, an untouched stretch of swamp and scrubby highland just where the Mississippi hill country drops off into the Delta. To the west is a sizable oxbow lake that is said to have been cutoff from the Ohio River eons ago. The fact that Bee Lake, as it's called, is a fishing destination with its own boat ramp and a modest marina seems to have had little or no effect on the slow degradation of Thornton.

Thornton proper consists of one block of unpainted clapboard buildings. There is some sort of store in one of them, a grocery-drygoods-hardware hybrid where, no matter what you've gone in looking for, you're likely to come out with beer.

In the course of my stay, I became blind to Thornton. The more I'd drive past it, the less I'd see it. Then one day I got held up in Indianola for longer than I'd intended and came onto Thornton later than I ever had before. The sun had just set, and Thornton's main street—Thornton's only street—was packed with people. Men almost without exception. Black men without exception. The neighborly esprit de corps I'd sensed on John Woods's street was sadly lacking in Thornton. There was no drunkenness to speak of, little in the way of animation, certainly no joy, just idle aimlessness. People—lots of people—merely standing around.

Home from work, some of them. Out of work, many of them. And at the sort of loose ends the Delta seems to insist on. It's a make-your-own-fun sort of place. If there's a functioning Cineplex in the Delta, I don't know where it is, and as an indication of the stark otherworldliness of the region, I can say with certainty that in the entire Mississippi Delta, all seven thousand square miles, there is but one Starbucks.

Seeing the citizens of Thornton milling around at sunset, I was put immediately in mind of Lucas McCarty most any afternoon. Bored, exasperated, hemmed in by geography generally and his disability specifically, Lucas is routinely obliged to amuse himself. The opportunities and employment prospects for Lucas and people like him remain scant and restricted.

In the summer of 2007, I attended with Lucas an employment conference for augmented communicators held in Pittsburgh. Virtually everyone there was obliged to use some form of communication device, chiefly due to complications from cerebral palsy.

My leading memory of that three-day conference is how very long everything took. Every question. Every response. Every presentation. Every meal. Every shift in venue. Every programming wrinkle. Everything. To live with a disability like cerebral palsy is to live in slow motion. Nothing is easy, particularly making yourself understood. I saw enormous ingenuity on display—creative uses of hardware and technology that allowed for toe typers and head pointers and laser dot users to communicate more readily than they otherwise might have—but there's no such thing as a quick and wholly unlabored chat with an augmented communicator.

Combine that with the attendant motor challenges of living with CP, and it's little surprise that the unemployment rate among people like Lucas McCarty is a whopping 85 percent. Though I arrived at the conference expecting some sort of specialized job fair, this was a different sort of gathering entirely, an extended opportunity for the airing of hopes, frustrations, idle plans, maddening setbacks, and the occasional painfully bad joke—nearly all expressed with the arid, androidal precision of the prevailing synthetic voice known as Perfect Paul.

Given his restricted opportunities in an able-bodied world, Lucas's weekly visits to a holiness church have come to impress me as entirely sensible. One Sunday when the olive oil comes out and Bishop Knighten wades into the congregation, who's to say Lucas McCarty won't rise and walk?

Ebony Elvis

In the first months after I'd met Lucas, when we were riding around the Delta, we had a few scattershot theological conversations. They were chiefly in the who's-going-to-hell-and-for-what-exactly vein. We never specifically talked about what went on at Trinity. I'd attended the church a half dozen times by then and so was acquainted with the emphasis on miracles and healing. I'd also heard enough testimony from people who'd found relief through prayer to assume that while Lucas certainly enjoyed the congregation's unqualified acceptance, he might also have kept showing up in hopes of being made whole and right.

Then I began to have conversations with various of Trinity's members, long leisurely chats away from the church where I could ask what I pleased and they could tell me what they liked. Soon enough I'd arrived at a fresh understanding of the ministry. On one level, the Trinity House of Prayer is home to accomplished gospel music, monumentally long sermons, and praise that frequently crowds hysteria. But closer to its core, and less obvious to a visitor like me, Trinity traffics in a brand of gradual, hard-won redemption.

At my childhood church, new members usually came via Westinghouse transfers. Well-scrubbed families traded their churches in Houston or Wichita for ours. At the

Trinity House of Prayer new members straggle in from grimmer regions. They tend to be freshly reformed alcoholics, recovering addicts, all-purpose backsliders who have arrived by plan or by chance within the orbit of Bishop Knighten and have yielded to the claims of his considerable gravity. The bishop is the sort of shepherd content to prod and nudge his flock unless he sees the need to raise his staff and crack a head or two.

On that stormy night in his front room, John Woods recalled his first glimpse of Willie B. Knighten. Woods was a child at the time, and the bishop was in his late teens. "They used to call him Sonny," Woods told me, "and he loved to fight. I saw him knock a guy out. They were behind a cafe on a Sunday evening with boxing gloves on. It was the bishop and a fellow called Mule. The bishop hit him once—*boom*—and laid him out cold."

That memory was very much with John Woods years later at one of Bishop Knighten's revivals. Woods was far from saved at the time. "I was smoking cigarettes and trying to quit," he said. "The bishop had a prayer line, and I got in it. It was getting shorter and shorter, and when the bishop got to me, he asked if I'd quit smoking. I told him yes. I *lied* in the prayer line in the house of God. Lied to Sonny Knighten." John Woods quaked a little at the memory of it.

Bishop Knighten's physical fearlessness, his toughness, have persisted into his seventh decade, and he remains a man who shies from no one. There is no sinner afoot on God's green earth Sonny Knighten wouldn't try to bring to the Lord. Accordingly, the congregation of the Trinity House of Prayer is salted with reclamation projects, people who have climbed out of deep, dark holes thanks to a hand up from the bishop. One such is Danny Fairley, Trinity's virtuoso guitar player.

From my first Sunday at the Trinity House of Prayer, I'd been curious about Danny. He is a large, broad-shouldered man in his midfifties who fairly dwarfs his guitar. His ivory Stratocaster looks like a child's toy in his hands and seems at comedic odds with Fairley's menacing appearance. Danny sat just behind me during my maiden exposure to a Bishop Knighten sermon, and I distinctly remember his growling interjections of "Yes, Lord!" and "My God!" whenever the bishop made stirring ecclesiastical sense or the spirit simply moved him.

He made me nervous—with his size and his scowl and his gold tooth. Danny struck me as the sort who, given the provocation, could readily break a guy like me in half. When the service ended and we all stood, I felt his ten-pound hand on my shoulder. He was smiling, welcoming, gentle. This was the Danny I would come to know.

By profession Danny Fairley is a plumber and electrician, and I arranged to meet him one afternoon at a house he was working on, a place barely framed up and under roof in a field west of Indianola. The large lot was treeless and windswept. It held the promise of the brand of pasture living that has become common not just in the Delta but throughout the South. At least Delta residents have a handy excuse.

The lush, unbroken hardwood forest that covered the place a century and a half ago—thick with American elms, ash, and Nuttall oaks—has long since been timbered and swept away. Only a protected swath of national forest remains west of Yazoo City. The balance of the Delta's woodlands was either clear cut for farming or harvested to fuel steam-driven paddle wheelers on the Mississippi, each capable of burning thirty cords of hardwood a day.

Danny and his helper were busy roughing in a bathtub when I pulled up. They were boring holes and gluing pipe as the wind blew trash and grit through the unfinished window openings and tore relentlessly at the white house wrap. Danny led me to a sheltered spot around back where the patio had yet to be laid, and we each parked on a stack of block to talk.

At the time, I was still trying to sort out who was who at Trinity, and Danny helped by identifying about half the congregation as his relations. He told me his wife, Ruthie, served as one of the white-coated church ushers while his sister, Kathy, sang in the choir and made announcements every week. The choir director/organist—sixteen-year-old Aundre—turned out to be Danny's grandson. The drummer, Cord, was his nephew.

For his part, Danny had started attending Trinity in 1989. "On a Friday night," he told me, and I could tell by his expression that he'd come a long way to get there.

Danny Fairley grew up poor in the Delta. He lived in a house just down the dirt road from where Lucas's grandfather's catfish ponds are located today. Danny and his brother Tommy shared an interest in music but had no means between them to purchase an actual guitar. "We nailed a string and a Pet Milk can to the wall," Danny recalled, "and we played on that one string for a while. Then we put up two strings so we could make chords. We eventually got an antifreeze can, put a stick down in it, and made a guitar out of that."

It served well enough to be strummed in public for pay. "Tommy used to go to the Yellow Dog Cafe in Moorhead," Danny told me, "and he'd play for a bunch of farmers there. On Saturdays, I'd go with him, and we'd both play that two-string antifreeze can. After a while, we made enough money to buy a real guitar. It cost seventeen dollars."

Because it was mostly Tommy's money, it was mostly Tommy's guitar, which wouldn't have mattered except that Tommy was left-handed and Danny wasn't. "When he'd go to school, I'd turn the strings around, and he'd come home and beat me up," Danny said. "So I learned how to play the thing bottom upwards. When I finally got my personal guitar, I had to learn it all over again. But it was in my head and in my heart to do it."

Like many musicians, Danny was partly inspired by the leading extra-musical feature of guitar virtuosity. "I could see whenever my brother played his guitar, all of the girls gathered around," Danny recalled. "That's what I wanted. I played in school every chance I got, and couldn't nobody tell me I wasn't the black Elvis Presley."

Danny got married at sixteen. He fathered two children and played in rock and roll bands that worked across the Delta and throughout the state. One of Danny's more memorable ensembles was the Golden Heartbreakers, a band consisting of four Fairley brothers and John Woods. Woods played bass once Danny had taught him how to. "We traveled all around the Delta," Danny said. "Metcalf, Greenville, Grenada—we had it sewn up around here."

A stint with the Mod Magicians followed, but with a family to raise, music yielded to more practical demands, and Danny took farm work as a tractor driver in addition to hiring out occasionally to his brother's plumbing business. It was along about this time that Danny Fairley started to drink, "drinking heavy," he told me. He grew unreliable and found it difficult to hold a job, even with his brother. "I became an alcoholic," Danny said, "and I lost my wife, my family."

He caught on at a fish farm but was fired from that job when he began to have seizures. "I was falling out," Danny recalled. "I didn't know where I was." Things just went south from there. "For fourteen years I drank heavy every day," Danny confessed. "Straight gin. They call it bumpy face." That would be Seagrams, so named for its textured bottle.

Drunk and nearly destitute, Danny Fairly stumbled upon Bishop Knighten one afternoon at a Moorhead service station. "He told me God had put me on his mind," Danny said. "I remember saying, 'You can't tell me when to be saved. I'll tell you.'"

Looking back, Danny figures now he *had* to be drunk to talk to Sonny Knighten that way. "I used to be scared of him," Danny allowed. "We all were. You didn't know if he was a secret agent or what. He dressed in black all the time, and the man's got some funny looking eyes. He could put the fear in you."

Twenty-four hours later, Danny met up with the bishop again, this time in dramatically eroded circumstances. "I'd gone into a blind stagger," Danny told me. "I couldn't see anything and couldn't walk. The bishop came down to my house and laid his hands on me. He prayed for me. That Friday night I started to church, and I've been there ever since. No drinks. No seizures. No cigarettes. Nothing since then."

After a few months in the pews, Danny began to sit in with the Trinity band. He found a musical foil in the church's bass player, Anthony Clark. "The choir rehearses," Danny said, "but me and Brother Clark don't. When they start playing, then we know what to play." Though Danny insists his guitar "don't play blues no more—it just plays gospel," there's often a spirited byplay between Danny and Brother Clark that verges on extra-ecclesiastical. Maybe not blues outright, but awfully close.

During the opening hour of service, when music dominates, Danny occupies a stool hard by the back sanctuary door where Lucas enters and exits Sunday after Sunday. It was from this perch that he first laid eyes on Lucas in 1996. "I'll never forget that day," Danny told me. "Brother John Woods came in, and I saw him holding the door, and then this little fellow came in on his knees." Lucas would have been ten years old at the time. "He was the happiest thing you'd want to see. He came in shouting. There I sat worried about what tomorrow might bring, and this little boy, walking on his knees, was as happy as he could be."

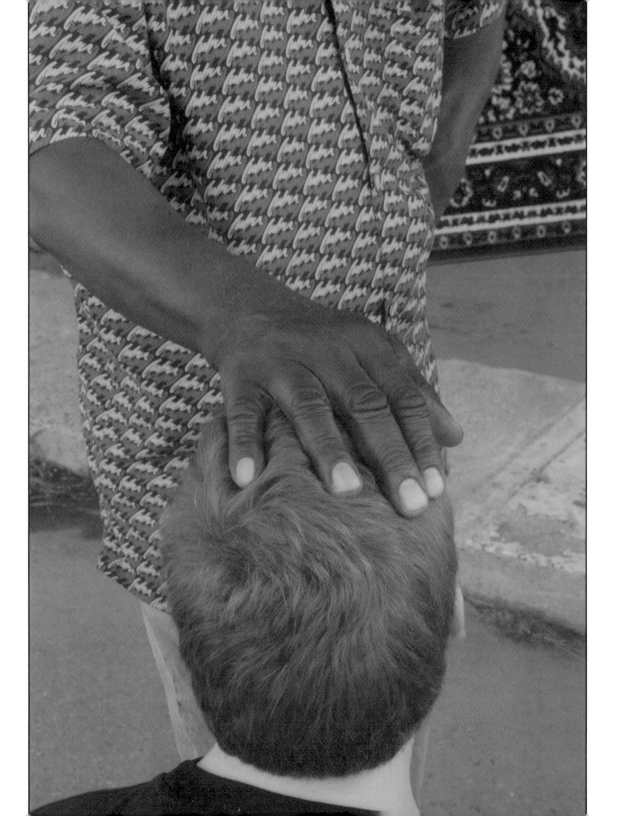

I Didn't Know Sin Was So Heavy

It took me a while to catch up with the bishop outside of the church. Our exchanges in the sanctuary were always cordial but brief. For a man who could preach extemporaneously for three hours, the bishop seemed restrained if not aloof away from the pulpit, even six feet away from the pulpit. In my visits to the House of Prayer, I'd come away with a pretty good read on the drift of Bishop Knighten's theology, but I had only a secondhand sense of him as a man, and much of what I had been told struck me as a little too vague and unreliable to put much stock in.

People I'd spoken to, white people almost exclusively, had passed along gossipy nuggets about the bishop. I'd been assured the bishop owned a string of liquor stores, was informed he'd been in a gang and had been obliged to leave the state for a decade in order to avoid arrest. I'd been told the bishop routinely plundered church coffers for his own use and was about as holy as a light pole, if I wanted to know the truth.

I still don't know for a fact if Bishop Willie B. Knighten is a Delta liquor store magnate, but having talked to him now at length and having spent some time around him, I can't for the life of me imagine he'd have the time to be one to much effect. The bishop oversees his own modest denomination. The Trinity House of Prayer is the flagship sanctuary of a loose confederation of seven churches. Most of them are located in the Delta, but one is up in Southhaven, a suburb of Memphis in northernmost Mississippi.

Bishop Knighten routinely travels the circuit, tending his ever-expanding flock. He delivers sermons when invited by the presiding pastors and is in direct charge of two congregations on his own. One attends the Trinity House of Prayer in Moorhead while the other, newer and far more fledgling, is attached to a church in Greenville that the bishop recently engineered the purchase of. Formerly a Congregationalist church, the brick building is traditional in design with a proper steeple, a standard-issue Protestant sanctuary, and a fellowship hall.

It's located just off the main east-west drag into Greenville, and I arrived there a quarter hour early for an appointment with Bishop Knighten to find Anthony Clark waiting for me. Aside from being Trinity's bass player, Clark is married to the bishop's niece, Hermenia, and is about as deeply involved in the life of the church as a member could be. Professionally, Anthony Clark is in the home security business, a thriving trade in the Delta. Thievery, as it turns out, is the leading blight of the place.

Anthony's brother, Michael Clark, has long been a police officer in the area, and a brief chat with him on one of my first Delta visits quickly disabused me of almost everything I'd read about the region and crime. From outside looking in, news of gang infiltration—in Greenville primarily—tends to both dominate the headlines and eclipse the homelier fact that the Delta is chiefly a place where things of any value get gone.

"We've got a lot of theft," Michael Clark told me. "Residential burglaries, property theft, auto theft. They might have more drug-related issues in Greenville, but out in the rest of the Delta, that's not our biggest problem." While serving in Indianola, Michael Clark once answered a call to the home of Jimmy and Joanne Lear, Lucas's grandparents. Someone had broken into their house and stolen not just Joanne's silver but all of Jimmy's Ole Miss memorabilia from his playing days. Jimmy was the quarterback of the undefeated 1952 Sugar Bowl team. Anthony Clark got called in shortly thereafter in a bid to protect everything else fit to tempt a thief. This is an all too common story in the Delta.

I remember attending a tent revival/gospel music marathon with Lucas on a ninety-degree May afternoon. My job was to keep pouring water into him, so I was hanging close to Lucas at the lip of the stage. That left me handy to hear the testimony from sinners in the prayer line. They would pass by, thanking Jesus for one thing or another, and I was struck at the time by how many gave praise for being kept by the sweet Lord from stealing.

These are just the people the bishop is trying to reach with his ministry while protecting church property from them until he does, a delicate predicament for a man of God with seven houses of worship. When I arrived at the new addition in Greenville, Anthony Clark gave me a quick tour of the place. As we wandered from the sanctuary to the church offices to what will soon be a preschool, I asked Anthony about his uncle by marriage and was told that Willie B. Knighten is an interior decorator by trade.

The man himself arrived a few minutes later, and we all retired to his office, where he parked behind his desk and asked me, "What do you want to hear? My life story?" All I had to tell him was, "Yes."

I was born about a mile out from Sunflower. My father worked a lot of land, leased a lot of land—called standing rent. I was the last of twelve kids. I've got nieces and nephews older than me.

We plowed mules and ran a lot of cows and hogs. I had to see about all that livestock and pump water, and I got tired of it. I'd been kicked out of school. The teachers used to pass me up to get me out of their classrooms. I got all the the way to the sixth grade, but I've got about a third-grade education.

When I was fifteen I caught a ride on a truck going to North Carolina. I worked on a tobacco farm in Swansboro, across from Fort Bragg. That would have been 1955, '56. I went all across the state.

I left there when the harvest was over and went to Florida.

To Homestead, and then from there to New York state before I came back to Mississippi.

When I was young, I had a corrupted appendix, and the doctor did surgery. They didn't think they'd be able to save me. It didn't look good, but I always felt I had a choice—get well and serve God or die like I was. When the doctor couldn't do anymore, I surrendered to God.

I didn't like to promise God nothing if I wasn't going to do it. After I'd make God a promise, I'd try for a while, but the people at the churches I was going to weren't faithful. They were in church on Sunday but partying the rest of the time, so I'd soon find myself back in the world.

67

One Christmas Eve—this would have been 1964 when I was twenty-three—me and some boys went to a gambling house to stick it up. We had one gun with no bullets in it, and I was the one that got trapped in there with that empty gun.

One of my guys messed up the robbery. I told them to put all those boys up against the wall and take their weapons before they went after the money. But this guy was raking money off the table, and he gave them the opportunity. The bullets started flying.

My cousin got shot in the back. The bullet went through his lungs. By the time we got him to the car, he was bleeding out of his nose and mouth, out of his ears. The fellow driving ran the car off the road, and everybody else got out and ran, but I couldn't leave my cousin.

I got behind the wheel, and I was trying to make it back to Sunflower, trying to get my partner to the hospital, but I got lost. My cousin fell over in my lap. I kind of figured he was dead, but I didn't want to think he was dead. I took him home. His brother-in-law came out, and I told him what had happened.

Then I carried his body to the police station and turned myself in. They handcuffed me, and the next day they brought some of the other guys in.

The farmer who had the gambling house didn't want to come and testify. My lawyer wanted me to plead guilty to seventeen years in the state penitentiary. I stayed in jail for three months before the trial in circuit court. I pled out, and the deputy sheriff, who had good influence with the judge, asked him to give me a county sentence.

He wanted to keep me in his jail because I'd brought a body in. He told the judge, and I'll never forget this, "I like a nigger with nerve." I didn't care what he called me as long as I stayed out of Parchman.

They gave the other guys three years probation. The judge turned around and gave me six months in the county jail. They sold me another six months for five hundred dollars. If I couldn't come up with the money, I'd serve a year. It was two years probation after that.

I got married, moved to Chicago, and worked with a bricklayer there for a few years. Me and my brother set up our own little grocery store and service station. I got to clowning and acting the fool. Then the good Lord saved me.

I guess God's been dealing with me since I was about ten years old. I tried a number of times to get saved, because I knew God was always chasing me. I did all right in Chicago for about three years.

I'd go to a club, and people were drinking and partying and all this stuff, and I could hear the voice of God talking to me, saying, "They could get to fighting up in here, and you could catch the first bullet and go straight to hell."

That would bother me, and I'd get nervous. I even got to the place where I could hardly sleep. I thought people were after me. Then one night I hit my wife. Her face was all swollen, and I said, "That's it." I asked my brother if I could go to church with him. He was going to a little storefront church, but I didn't like the way the people carried on.

Then I woke up one morning before day, and I went into a trance. In a vision I saw Jesus coming, and He passed me up because I wasn't saved. I couldn't pray fast enough, and I was running behind Jesus and praying, but He was getting away. I started screaming and hollering, and that's when I snapped out of it. That thing shook me up.

Soon after that, I went to this storefront church. They had a missionary there, an old lady from Raleigh, North Carolina. She was running a revival. That woman laid hands on me, and it felt like the weight of a thousand pounds fell off of me. I didn't know sin was so heavy. I felt light, and I knew what was missing from my life from that moment.

I didn't fully know what I was seeking, but I knew I needed to have it.

I went to visit my mother in Mississippi, and I rode with a cousin over to Greenville to a club. A guy named Ted Taylor was playing the blues, and I was sitting there with a soda. A girl wanted to dance, and nobody around the table could dance but me, so I went and danced with that girl, and when I sat back down, that weight came back. When I got back to Chicago, I couldn't wait until they had another revival.

This was in 1970, and that revival was in its second week. It was done. All of the preaching was over. Everybody had their hats and coats. They were going home, but I said, "God, I ain't leaving here like this."

At that moment I found out what giving up was, when you give your inner self. When you want salvation more than you want your life. I just looked up toward heaven and spoke in tongues for about five minutes. Then the spirit of the Lord came into me. The sweetness of God came rushing in.

I didn't even feel human. I felt like I could float in the air. The glory of God was in that place.

I started preaching in Mississippi in 1974. I started running revivals, and I'd go into any church. Denomination didn't matter. Then I rented a storefront in Moorhead, and I ran a revival out of there. After a few weeks, we had two hundred people in there.

At Trinity, at all our churches, we're building the Kingdom. I appreciate visitors coming from other churches, but that's not where my focus is. I want the fallen. Jesus says, "He that's well don't need a doctor." I want the sick. I tell people all the time, "You need to tear up your agenda. The Lord's not working for us. We're working for Him."

Our churches are sanctified. We're not Pentecostal. Sanctification isn't a denomination. It's a way of life. At the Trinity House of Prayer, we believe in the full gospel. Father, Son, and the Holy Ghost.

Lucas tells me he likes my preaching. He says I keep my foot on the devil's head.

The Boats

In February of 2007, to celebrate his twenty-first birthday, Lucas McCarty went to the boats. That is Mississippi parlance for the casinos that have sprouted up on the Gulf coast and along the great river as a result of a special session of the state legislature in 1990. The proceedings were marked by a blend of economic desperation and institutional cowardice. A legislator from Natchez introduced a bill to allow riverboat gambling in his impoverished district. Its chances seemed laughable until other representatives from river communities and coastal counties began to sign onto the proposition that state-sanctioned gaming was their last, best hope for an economic rebound.

At the time, the region had quite a lot of rebounding to do. On a 1985 visit to the Sugar Ditch Alley neighborhood of the northern Delta community of Tunica, the Reverend Jesse Jackson had searingly branded the place "America's Ethiopia." Sugar Ditch's housing was deplorably substandard by any measure, and the neighborhood's open sewer—in late twentieth-century America—branded Sugar Ditch decisively third world.

By 1990, the state of the state was sufficiently dire to convince politicians they had to do something daring and controversial by way of remedy (while remaining as blameless as possible). Accordingly, the bill that permitted casinos in Mississippi was passed in the middle of the night and was marked by the sort of invertebrate dodges that elected officials the world over prefer to call "principled compromises."

The Mississippi legislature had a sanctimony problem. To say the state is socially conservative verges on euphemistic. Mississippi only got around to repealing Prohibition in 1966, so legislators were rightly fearful of their constituents' potential reaction to state-sanctioned gambling, a pursuit perfumed with Old Testament sulfur. They sought to soften the blow with a welter of caveats and risible stipulations.

Chief among them was that the gaming—it was never called "gambling," only "gaming"—would be confined to barges and riverboats afloat on either the Gulf of Mexico or the Mississippi River. That way actual games of chance would never be conducted on the sacred soil of the state of Mississippi. Sort of. While casinos in Biloxi, at Vicksburg, and Greenville, were placed on more or less actual barges, a novel approach was taken in Tunica. Canals, glorified ditches really, were dug well inland from the river to allow water into basins that were then sealed. Casino hotels were constructed on adjacent dry land while the actual gambling operation was left to float in the basin. Or at least touch it. Or closely crowd the vicinity of it.

As it turned out, the politicians had nothing to fear. The year 1992 saw the opening of the first Tunica casino, a place called Splash. It was packed every night, notwithstanding the $10 charge at the door just to get in. Today Mississippi casinos collectively rank closely behind Las Vegas and Atlantic City as national gaming profit centers, and they contribute around $200 million a year in state tax revenue.

The arcane circumstances of the industry's birth in Mississippi were revisited in the wake of Hurricane Katrina in 2005. At the height of the storm's violence, several of Biloxi's casino barges were flung on shore where they battered or destroyed outright much of Biloxi's developed waterfront. A fair amount of national head scratching followed along with embarrassing questions about the sanity of housing casinos on massive floating barges in the first place.

The legislature responded with a bill that was signed into law by the governor. Today in the state of Mississippi, gambling is allowed by statute to creep 800 yards inland. No ditches, no basins, no barges required.

Lucas made his birthday pilgrimage to Tunica with his father where, like most of the rest of his colleagues in vice, he lost money. That was surely painful for Lucas because he is as fond of money as anybody I've ever met. Lucas started his own house cleaning business a couple of summers ago, which happily combined his love for getting paid with his near obsession with tidiness. He managed to scare up a handful of clients, only a few of them blood relatives, but Indianola is hardly a housekeeper's paradise, and the work proved too erratic for Lucas to keep reliable help.

When there's occasion, Lucas is employed by Prentke Romich (the manufacturers of his communication device) as an ambassador for Minspeak. In that capacity, he frequently attends conferences in the fields of speech language pathology and assisted communication technology to demonstrate the capabilities of his Pathfinder in the hands of an accomplished user. When I met Lucas, his Prentke Romich contact and traveling companion was John Halloran of Little Rock. A speech therapist by training, Halloran is evangelical about the power of Minspeak to give unfettered voice to the voiceless, and his presentations at industry trade shows and academic conclaves tend to be wonders of dynamic persuasion.

More specifically, John Halloran is a devoted advocate of a kind of muscle memory, what he calls motor planning, as the means of unlocking fluency in assisted communicators. To his way of thinking, an accomplished Minspeak user is much like a piano virtuoso in that he knows instinctively which keys to press in which combination to produce the result he desires. With practice, according to Halloran, communicating on a Pathfinder can become little short of automatic.

While John's presentations are rich in video evidence illustrating his philosophy, he's never without a user or two to bring home the communicative power of motor planning. Occasionally, Lucas is one of his assistants, but more routinely John can be found in the company of Bac Shelton. Now in his midthirties, Bac is the son of a Vietnamese national and an American G.I. His cerebral palsy is of a milder sort than Lucas's. Bac's symptoms are largely confined to his upper body, but like Lucas, Bac is incapable of forming the words to speak.

Other than that, I would say Bac is perfectly normal except that his college degree, his talent as a painter, and his wicked sense of humor put him decidedly north of normal, not just in the sphere of cerebral palsy but in the world at large. Bac is that increasingly rare commodity in this life: a sport.

To see Bac and Lucas side by side is to witness the vagaries of chance. Complications at birth have impaired them both but to emphatically different degrees. With a bit more oxygen sooner, Bac would likely be telling his off-color jokes in his own voice and Lucas

77

could lose his kneepads and wander the world like Bac does now. I can't help but believe, however, that the fundamental personality traits that make Lucas Lucas and Bac Bac would remain unaltered. Bac is meticulous—in manner and dress—and a little self-effacing. Lucas is willful and can be selectively indifferent to appearances.

I once came across their Pathfinders sitting side by side on a table in a hotel ballroom. The condition of each was so revealing that they might as well have had name tags on them. Lucas's machine is always a bit of a mess. He isn't especially careful with it. It's dinged up, and there are crumbs and leavings in the key guard and the various recesses. Understandably, it tends to be drool splattered, and pretty frequently its battery is threatening to go dead. When its charge is weak, a Pathfinder cuts loose with an intermittent alarm that sounds like the siren on a French police car. Lucas is serenely capable of ignoring the racket altogether.

Bac's unit looks to have just come out of the box. It's equipped with an optional stand that tilts the keyboard for easier access and an adjustable visor that helps cut the glare on the LCD screen. When he's on the move, Bac carries his pathfinder carefully packed away in a knapsack. Lucas's unit can usually be found on his lap, on the floor, on his kitchen counter or—if he's kneewalking—in the possession of whomever happens to be at hand.

Bac types with his left pinky. Since his muscles aren't so contracted and involved as Lucas's, Bac is a relatively quick and decisive typist. He is readily capable of the ruthless dig or the salty quip, and he has customized his Pathfinder with a smattering of adult language for those occasions when only that sort of thing will do. Lucas's vocabulary, while scrupulously clean, is colorful, colloquial, and relentlessly inventive.

Conversing with Lucas and Bac is very much like chatting with anybody else, if only a bit more slowly. That's both a tribute to their talent with Minspeak and proof, John Halloran would insist, of the potent communicative power of Bruce Baker's language and motor planning in combination. If the holy grail for the speechless is real-time communication, the Pathfinder allows deft users like Bac and Lucas to cozy up fairly close to that mark. They both make use of the telephone readily (what's more real-time than that?), and Lucas is a common and enthusiastic presence on CB channels in the Indianola region.

As a layman, I find it curious that sales of Minspeak devices are far eclipsed by sales of products featuring "concept-based phrase prediction" as their primary mode of communication. Minspeak is a word-based language, like English or Farsi or Tagalog, and the fluent

Minspeak user can convey, freely and spontaneously, virtually anything he pleases. Phrase prediction, on the other hand, is sure to be of more limited conversational scope. Such devices feature touch screens and depend upon dynamic displays—shifting sets of icons devoted to specific topics. There may be a page featuring words and phrases to be used at a birthday party, a page for ordering from a restaurant menu, a page appropriate to a baseball game or an outing at the beach. This is just the sort of approach to allow for superficial participation while frustrating ordinary, real-world exchanges.

Let's say I'm an accomplished Minspeak user, and we're having a chat about the preferred diet of silverback gorillas. You're suddenly reminded of a vegetarian meal you ate at a diner two weeks earlier and of the gentleman who slipped in beside you at the lunch counter to confide that he was from Alpha Centari. Because I'm using Minspeak, or more precisely because Minspeak is word based, I can follow your conversation and contribute to it, no matter how daft and scattershot it may be.

A reliance on "concept-based phrase prediction" would put me in different straits altogether. You mention gorillas, and I tap an icon on my home screen that takes to me to a screen devoted to animals. On that screen, depending on how I've customized my unit, I may have to tap an icon of a monkey to get to a fuller range of primates that may or may not include silverback gorillas and very likely won't put me in reach of any language about their diets. Worse still, those icons I do have to choose from tend to shift position from screen to screen, which means a lot of hunting and pecking on my part, sure to slow me down further.

So far I've said exactly squat while you're prattling on about your favorite outer galaxies. To keep up, I'd need to back out of my monkey topics and start all over again. To add anything pertinent, I'd probably have to call up my keyboard and begin typing, and why would I need a $7,000 device for that?

For Lucas and Bac, their Pathfinders serve as extensions of their personalities. Their ability to say anything quickly renders their lack of natural speech relatively inconsequential and opens the way to fuller participation in life. I recently attended a conference in Jackson, Mississippi, where John Halloran was representing Prentke Romich in the exhibition hall with Lucas's assistance. Lucas and John got into a running conversation about a trip they'd like to take, an RV tour of the country organized around presentations on the power of Minspeak. By way of advance planning, they decided to visit an RV dealership just south of town, and I rode with them.

My job was to help John hoist Lucas into the vehicles and confirm to the salesman that Lucas was indeed about to come into a sizable settlement, one sufficient to put a $300,000 mobile home within reach. That was John's story anyway. Lucas took it from there. He toured a half dozen of the behemoths, traveling the length of each on his knees. He quizzed the salesman about square footage, the capacity of the power plant, fuel efficiency (!), and he located in each unit a proper cubby for his CB while perched in the driver's seat and actively drooling on the Corinthian leather.

The salesman took him seriously. What choice did he have? He'd surely never seen anyone quite like Lucas, and with his Pathfinder Lucas could (and did) ask anything that popped into his head. After a couple of hours of scrupulous browsing, I returned to the conference hotel while John and Lucas paid a call on a Vicksburg casino in a bid to help that settlement along. At the blackjack table, with John's guidance, Lucas won $400.

Since then, Lucas has exhibited a passion for gambling that is, thankfully, held in reasonable check by his native frugality. He makes fairly regular trips to the boats in Greenville or Tunica where he occasionally wins a little but never loses a lot. I accompanied him once for a spot of blackjack and can safely say there's no more desolate place on earth than a Mississippi casino on a weekday afternoon. The prevailing aroma of stale smoke and spilled beer has a distinct frat house quality, and far too many of the patrons seem to go about their gambling with a grim desperation. They don't just hope to win; they need to win.

I wasn't allowed to help Lucas play unless I played myself, and somehow I managed to drop $100 while Lucas lost only $40. "He's got discipline," John Halloran told me when I asked him about Lucas's gambling. "He loves money too much not to know when to quit."

Too Much Joy

This past June I made what I suspected would be one of my last visits to the Trinity House of Prayer. The service was dedicated to Lucas, which made for a happy, overstuffed sanctuary on a day of colorblind celebration. The tone was joyful, a welcome shift from earlier in the spring when the bishop's mood had been dark and his sermons perfumed with apocalypse. Who could blame him? At the time, the price of gas was crowding $4 a gallon. There was talk of a global food shortage. Jobs in the Delta were, if anything, scarcer than they'd been the year before—even the usually bulletproof Viking Range Corporation of Greenwood had laid off employees.

The bishop had plowed up a garden plot behind the church where he intended to plant vegetables for the benefit of the entire congregation. From all I've seen, Willie Knighten takes the role of shepherd seriously and isn't satisfied to offer only counsel and spiritual advice. In the attached building behind the sanctuary, the House of Prayer has a kitchen where, on many Sundays, the church serves a full meal to the members (and to interlopers like me) for a scant $3 a plate in a bid to help church families keep healthy and whole.

The members repay the bishop's conscientious stewardship and guidance by tithing with dogged reliability, even when times are tough and money is tight. In the course of the initial offering each Sunday, installments are made on obligations, usually to Brother Ricardo. He stands at a lectern alongside the offering table marking payments against promises in a well-thumbed spiral notebook. He then retires, along with Deacons Groves and Minton, to a room off the narthex to tabulate and reconcile.

This is the work of church going at Trinity, the mechanics of keeping holy. The spirit of Trinity, however, is something else altogether. In too many of the churches I've known, Christian living is treated as a kind of dutiful sideline, but there is palpable happiness infusing worship in this Delta church that I, for one, find consoling.

Danny Fairley's wife, Ruthie, explained it all to me one afternoon by happenstance. Ruthie serves as an usher in the church, and she often accompanies the bishop when he wades into the congregation to lay on hands. I showed her one of the photographs Lang Clay had taken during Sunday service. In it he'd captured a pocket of the congregation in a bit of a state. People were frozen in mid-shout, mid-flail. One young man had crumpled to floor. There were obvious tears and stricken expressions.

Ruthie studied the photo and smiled. "Too much joy," she said.

As I write this, Lucas McCarty is twenty-two years and four months old and has grown into manhood. The Lucas I met on that first Sunday some two years ago was still a boy with a boy's impulses and a boy's obsessions.

At the time, Lucas had a kind of girlfriend, though certainly more in his mind than hers. They'd met during his last year or so of schooling in Tennessee, and she'd served as an able-bodied pal and companion for Lucas, who'd been heartbroken to leave her and return to Indianola. While she went on with her life, Lucas nursed his infatuation. He was fully in the throes of it when I met him, and he plagued the poor girl with phone calls. Lucas routinely begged me to drive him to Memphis, where she lived, so he might drop in on her at work.

I would say he was single-minded except that Lucas managed simultaneously to be obsessed with a gentleman named Lee Williams, a singer of no little renown in gospel circles. Lucas is a fervent gospel music fan. He has amassed a considerable collection of recordings which, except for the odd Billy Ray Cyrus CD, is devoted to gospel music and largely to Lee Williams and the QC's—a backup band that goes by the abbreviation for Quality Christians.

Lucas has been a Lee Williams fan for years, and photos taken of Lucas and Williams together at various gospel sings in Indianola are displayed prominently in Lucas's kitchen.

Lee Williams is a kind, elegant gentleman. I had occasion to speak with him before an open-air performance in the Delta, and he told me he was formerly a truck driver. He had enjoyed, he said, the solitude of long hours on the road.

I could readily imagine that. Lee Williams is a serene presence, and he commands the stage with a stillness that is unusual among gospel singers. Upon seeing Williams perform, I couldn't help but imagine part of the attraction for Lucas was Williams's calm assurance. He gives the impression of being all but metaphysically unexcitable. They are an odd pair, Williams and Lucas. The former Zen-like. The latter in fitful, spastic control of his rebellious body. I've grown to think Lucas is drawn less to Williams's music than to his peace. "Lee," Lucas told me once, "is like Jesus." It's less of a stretch than you might imagine.

But even Christ Himself would have wearied of the onslaught Lucas inflicted on Williams. Lucas had somehow come by Williams's home and cell numbers, and he would dial the man many times a day, leaving voicemail messages he'd pre-programmed into his Pathfinder. Lucas was evermore pleading to see Williams, to visit the man at his Tupelo home or secure a date when Williams might swing through Indianola and drop by for a visit. Understandably, Williams would go silent for weeks, waiting for the feverish phone calls to stop. Only then would he check in, but too often that would start the cycle all over again.

Between Lucas's compulsion to speak with Williams and his obsession with his Memphis "girlfriend," he tended toward a strain of simmering unhappiness and dissatisfaction. A year or so before I'd met him, Lucas's behavior had grown sufficiently unhinged and self-destructive to rate psychiatric intervention. Lucas wanted to die and said as much, threatened as much. When we were introduced, Lucas was on the mend, and in the time I've known him, I've watched Lucas McCarty grow to embrace a kind of peace.

I remember one morning early on in our acquaintance when Lucas was so frustrated and agitated over the state of his life that John Woods had to be called in to calm him down. "Lucas," John told him, "the only thing in this world you can control is yourself." Lucas might not have believed that then, but he has come to believe it since.

Today Lucas owns a pickup truck—CB equipped, of course—and his friends and family get recruited to drive him around in it. He works as a Prentke Romich ambassador when there's call for it and holds a job at his father's restaurant. He visits the boats every now and again in an agreeable, sporting sort of way. Upon meeting Lucas, I did him the

87

usual able-bodied disservice of silently wishing him normal. I couldn't yet see that he was already extraordinary.

Not getting to say what you want to say is hard. That's why I learned to talk. Now I work. I have a truck with a CB in it, and my grandmother, Go-Go, drives me around. I love my church, and I'd like a girlfriend, a nice girl I could hang out with and date. When people look at me, I want them to know I'm not just a boy in a chair.

Lucas McCarty sings in the choir of the Trinity House of Prayer in Moorhead, Mississippi, and that's the most remarkable thing I know.

Photographs

Acknowledgments

Lang and Tom would like to thank the many people who helped make this book possible. Lucas McCarty, his mother, Elizabeth, and the extended Lear and McCarty families. The clergy and congregation of the Trinity House of Prayer. Julie Chadwick and the staff and clients of the North Mississippi Regional Center in Oxford. Billy Chadwick of Oxford. John Halloran of Prentke Romich. Jamie Kornegay of Turnrow Books. Tra and Margaret Dubois of Leland, Mississippi, and the management and staff of the Alluvian Hotel in Greenwood.

On the publishing side, our gratitude goes out to our agent, Marian Young, and our editor/publisher, Ashley Gordon. Without their creativity and imagination, this book simply would not exist.

About the Author

T.R. PEARSON is the author of a dozen novels, including *A Short History of A Small Place* and *Blue Ridge*, and four works of nonfiction. He lives in Virginia.

About the Photographer

LANGDON CLAY was born in New York City and raised in New England. He photographs around the country and beyond for shelter magazines and coffee table books. The bulk of his commercial work involves architecture, interiors, gardens and food, featured in such publications as *Jefferson's Monticello* by Howard Adams and *From My Chateau Kitchen* by Anne Willan. His art photography can be found in museums in Paris, London, New York, Chicago, New Orleans, and Jackson, Mississippi. He resides on the banks of Cassidy Bayou in the little Delta town of Sumner, Mississippi, with his wife, photographer Maude Schuyler Clay, and three mostly grown children; Anna, Schuyler, and Sophie.

About the Publisher

Mockingbird Publishing partners with not-for-profit organizations on every book. A portion of the proceeds from *Year of Our Lord* will be donated to support the outreach programs of the Trinity House of Prayer and a foundation for Lucas McCarty.

LaVergne, TN USA
05 October 2010
199504LV00001B